10 Simple Steps to Improving Overall Financial Wellness

A quick-action reference guide for implementing basic personal financial strategies

K. Thomas Hutt, CFP®, CPA, MBA

authorHOUSE®

AuthorHouse™
1663 Liberty Drive
Bloomington, IN 47403
www.authorhouse.com
Phone: 1-800-839-8640

First published by AuthorHouse   11/21/2011

ISBN: 978-1-4670-3759-4 (sc)
ISBN: 978-1-4670-3758-7 (ebk)

Library of Congress Control Number: 2011916606

Printed in the United States of America

This book is printed on acid-free paper.

Dedication

To my family: Shelley, my wife; Sean, my eldest son; Kevin Jr., my son; Taylor, my daughter; and Donald II, my stepson. A man is truly blessed when he has a peaceful home life and a great family.

CONTENTS

10 Simple Steps to Improving
Overall Financial Wellness

Acknowledgments

To my wife and best friend, Shelley. Thanks for the joy you bring into my life as well as our family. To Sean, Kevin Jr., Taylor, and Donald II. You guys are truly amazing. You have achieved and exceeded my best wishes for your lives. I am so very proud of you guys.

To my hero, my role model, my dad, Louis G. Hutt Sr.—a man who modeled quiet strength and calm in the midst of the storms of life. Dad, you are my guiding strength and an example I follow every day of my life.

To my mother, Joyce Hutt, who often said, "Life is about principles." She professed them and raised her children by them. Mom, it is your principles that define my character to this day, and I now teach those principles to your grandchildren.

To my mentor and big brother, Louis G. Hutt, Jr. Thanks for being a shining example of what a young man like me could aspire to be. Thank you for coaching me to success.

To my spiritual mentor, my little sister, Tracee, who through her life has always demonstrated that God is in control. Thanks for your prayers. I have truly been blessed by them.

About the Author

Kevin Thomas Hutt is a certified financial planner and certified public accountant with over twenty-five years of experience in the financial-services industry. His financial advice has been featured numerous times on local television stations and in newspapers, as well as *Money* magazine, *Black Enterprise* magazine, *Heart & Soul* magazine, and PBS's *Moneywise* TV.

He began his career in public accounting with the regional firm of Bennett, Hutt & Company. He serves as the firm's partner in charge of corporate tax, accounting and consultant services. Kevin is also managing partner of Onyx Asset Management, LLC, an independent firm specializing in financial services for high net worth individuals, institutions and businesses.

Kevin has a long-standing commitment to public service. He serves as Treasurer of the Coppin State University Development Foundation in Baltimore, Maryland. He is a member of the Parents' Leadership Council for American University, Washington, DC. In the past he has served as Chairman of the Coppin Heights Community Development Corporation in Baltimore, Maryland.

Kevin is a graduate of St. Louis University where he received his Bachelor Science Degree in Accounting.

He received a Master Degree in Business Administration from Morgan State University.

Kevin is married with has three childern, a stepson and two grandchildren.

You can contact Kevin at:

Kevin T. Hutt, CFP®, CPA, MBA
PO Box 893
Columbia, MD 21044
kevin@simplymoney101.com

You can visit Kevin at:

www.simplymoney101.com

Introduction

Let me start by telling you what this book is not. It is not a guide on how to become a millionaire. It is not a guide on how to build wealth overnight. Bookstores are fully stocked with offerings on these topics.

The frank truth is that most people will never become millionaires. However, they can still take simple yet significant steps to improve their overall financial wellness.

What Is Financial Wellness?

Merriam-Webster Online (http://www.m-w.com) defines *wellness* as "the quality or state of being in good health especially as an **actively sought goal**." Synonyms are *healthiness, soundness, wholeness,* and *wholesomeness.* Antonyms are *illness, sickness, unhealthiness,* and *unsoundness.*

Merriam-Webster Online defines *financial* as "relating to finance." Synonyms are *fiscal* and *monetary.*

I believe that we all can improve our overall financial wellness. Anyone can stop being ill and unhealthy financially and improve his or her fiscal and monetary healthiness and wholesomeness.

Over my nearly thirty years as a certified financial planner and certified public accountant, I have had the pleasure of advising numerous clients on matters of personal finance. My experience has taught me that there are simple steps most of us can take to improve our financial wellness. These steps aren't necessarily sophisticated. On the contrary, the steps presented are rather fundamental and familiar.

I have encapsulated these steps into 10 Simple Steps to Improving Overall Financial Wellness. Surprisingly, the 10 Simple Steps are about doing the fundamentals well. These steps recap simple strategies that you probably already know can improve your financial wellness. Sadly, it has been my experience that many fail miserably at the basic fundamentals. The 10 Simple Steps consists of two parts:

➢ Ten steps that enhance and improve overall financial wellness
➢ The tenth step highlights "ten" common financial mishaps to avoid

The 10 Simple Steps are presented in what I call a "quick action" read format. This facilitates quick reading and quick implementation of suggested Action Steps.

I sincerely hope that this book proves to be an effective guide to improving your overall financial wellness.

All the best,

K. Thomas Hutt, CFP®, CPA, MBA

Simple Step #1:
Save for Retirement

Saving for retirement is the first and most critical step to improving overall financial wellness. A recent article in SmartMoneyAdvice.com highlighted some the following US retirement statistics:

Out of one hundred people who start working at the age of twenty-five, by age sixty-five:

- ➢ One is wealthy.
- ➢ Four have adequate capital stowed away for retirement.
- ➢ Three are still working.
- ➢ Sixty-three are dependent on Social Security, friends, relatives, or charity.
- ➢ Twenty-nine are deceased.

Out of one hundred people who start working at the age of twenty-five, by age sixty-five:

- ➢ One is financially independent, with assets approaching or exceeding $1,000,000, and does not need Social Security benefits at all.

> ➢ Two have adequate pension or retirement savings.
> ➢ Thirty-five retire with less than $100,000 and have some form of pension in addition to Social Security.
> ➢ Sixty-two retire with less than $25,000 in assets and depend on Social Security or family for their retirement.

The majority of Americans are *not* be financially secure in retirement.

Great American Risk Transfer

Most experts theorize that there is a looming retirement crisis in America. I believe this retirement crisis will disproportionately affect middle—to low-income Americans.

The good news is that Americans are living longer. The bad news is that employers can't afford it. Many are having difficulty setting aside sufficient resources to cover pension-benefit obligations for their employees who will now have an extended life expectancy. Many employers are converting to defined contribution plans—that is, 401(k) plans. Under such plans, the employer makes a current matching contribution to an employee retirement account. This matching contribution is less costly than contributing to a pension benefit plan for an employee. Once the employer meets its employer matching contribution, the employer is no longer responsible for the employee's retirement. The risk of retirement has been successfully transferred from the employer to the employee.

Retirement risk is defined as the probability of outliving retirement assets. To protect against such risk, sufficient resources must be saved to meet retirement needs.

Determining Retirement Needs

Below is an example of a simple approach used to estimate the amount of assets needed for retirement.

Assumptions
Annual gross wages: $50,000
Length of time until retirement age of 65: 20 years
Length of time in retirement: 20 years

(A) Retirement assets needed	
Annual gross wages:	$50,000
Less federal tax withholding @ 20 percent:	($10,000)
Less state tax withholding @ 7 percent:	($3,500)
Less Social Security tax withholding @ 6.2 percent:	($3,100)
Less Medicare tax withholding @ 1.45 percent:	($725)
Annual after-tax income:	$32,675
Estimated percentage needed in retirement:	75 percent
Annual retirement-income need:	$24,506
Multiplied by number of years in retirement:	20
Total retirement assets needed (A):	*$490,120*

(B) Amount expected from Social Security
Estimated annual Social Security: $13,200
Multiplied by number of years
    expected to receive benefits: <u>20</u>
       Total assets from Social Security (B):   *$264,000*

(C) Additional retirement assets needed
    (A minus B):   <u>*$226,120*</u>

Determining the Amount of Monthly Savings Required

Additional retirement assets needed: $226,120
Divided by number of years
remaining before retirement: <u>20</u>
Annual savings need: $ 11,306
Divide by twelve for monthly
    savings need: <u>$942</u>

[See Appendix 1 for a blank Retirement Analysis Worksheet.]

Accumulating Retirement Assets

Three factors contribute toward the accumulation and growth of retirement assets—that is, savings:

1) Time (the period over which money is saved)
2) Investment amount (the amount contributed toward periodically)
3) Investment return (the annual growth on savings and investment income earned)

These three elements have an inverse relationship. The more there is of one element, the less need there is for the others. For example, the more time you have to save, the less you need to contribute on a periodic basis. On the other hand, the less time you have to save, the more you need to contribute to retirement on a periodic basis. If there is less time to save, there may also be a need for a greater return on investment.

Conclusion

Retirement is the ultimate report card on how financial affairs were managed during the working years. It is never too late to start saving for retirement. Taking the suggested Action Steps below may not make you rich, but they will most certainly improve your long-term financial wellness by minimizing retirement risks.

Start today!

Action Steps to Improve Financial Wellness

1) Begin immediately! Take advantage of time. That is the most important factor in saving for retirement. Once time is lost, it cannot be recovered.

2) Enroll in your employer's retirement plan and start having savings withheld *each and every* pay period.

3) Determine if your employer offers a matching contribution and contribute an amount at least equal to that matching amount.

4) If your employer does not provide a retirement plan, or you have not met the eligibility requirements, open an Individual Retirement Account (IRA) and have a retirement savings amount deducted from your bank account every pay period.

5) Calculate your retirement need in order to determine the required monthly savings amount. If unable to meet the requirement get as close as reasonable. Having something for retirement is better than nothing.

Simple Step #2: Maintain a Family Emergency Management Account

Over your lifespan, over your earning years, over your day-to-day life, the unexpected can be expected to happen. You can count on an emergency or two or three—job loss, disability, troubled pregnancy and no maternity leave left, and so on.

Maintaining a Family Emergency Management Account (FEMA) is critical to overall financial wellness. With a FEMA, when a financial emergency arises, there will be less of a need to redeem retirement savings or incur additional debt. Redeeming retirement assets unexpectedly could derail progress toward saving for retirement. Having a FEMA is a defensive strategy that allows you to protect yourself against unexpected financial emergencies that could cause financial upheaval.

Conventional wisdom suggests an emergency savings account equal to three to six months of living expenses. Of course, this is the gold standard, and it is often difficult to set aside that much. However, having something set aside for emergencies is far better than nothing.

Conclusion

Prepare for the unexpected so that progress toward improving overall financial wellness is not suddenly derailed by an emergency. By committing to set aside monies for emergenices it can be quite surprising and refreshing to see how fast the FEMA grows over a short period of time.

Action Steps to Improve Financial Wellness

1) Create a budget line-item for funding the FEMA.

2) Attempt to save 3-6 months of living expenses as an emergency reserve.

3) Set up a systematic savings plan to fund a FEMA.

4) Set up the ability to easily transfer money from the FEMA back to the checking account when needed.

5) Commit to making withdraws from the FEMA only in the case of the most severe emergencies.

Simple Step #3:
Buy Risk Protection

Insurance is an instrument that provides risk protection against a loss that would be incurred upon the occurrence of a certain event.

Life Insurance

One of the fundamental purposes of life insurance is to provide protection against the loss of income that would occur upon the death of a family member, generally one whose lost income would harm the dependent family's financial situation. Upon that individual's death, the insurance company would provide a financial death benefit to beneficiaries, usually family members. This death benefit should help to replace the loss of income from the deceased person.

Insuring children is not a concern because they don't provide income and support to the family, unless the child is music artist or actor. For adults who contribute significantly to the household income, failure to buy life insurance could result in severe economic hardship for the surviving family members. Below are just a few examples:

- ➤ Family members can no longer afford to meet debt obligations, such as a mortgage payment or car payments.
- ➤ Family members can no longer afford normal living expenses.
- ➤ Family members can no longer pay for the children's education.
- ➤ The spouse can no longer afford to retire.
- ➤ Family members may not even have the resources for a funeral.

Determining the Amount of Life Insurance Needed

Assumptions

Husband's annual wage: $50,000

Wife's annual wage: $40,000

Two children, ages two and one

Projected college cost: $40,000/yearly per child;

Total Cost of College for both children: $320,000

Husband estimated life insurance need:

(A) Income replacement need

Annual gross wages:	$50,000
Less federal tax withholding @ 20 percent:	($10,000)
Less state tax withholding @ 7 percent:	($3,500)
Less Social Security tax withholding @ 6.2 percent:	($3,100)
Less Medicare tax withholding @ 1.45 percent:	($725)
Annual after-tax income:	$32,675

Estimated percentage needed by family members:	x<u>75 percent</u>
Annual retirement income need:	$24,506
Multiplied by number of years until youngest child is age 21:	<u>20</u>
Total replacement income needed (A):	*<u>$490,120</u>*

(B) Funeral and estate administration need

Funeral expense:	$15,000
Estate administration:	<u>$10,000</u>
Total funeral and estate administration need (B):	*$ 25,000*

(C) Debt payoff need

Mortgage balance:	$250,000
Credit-card balances:	$20,000
Auto loan balances:	$25,000
Other debts:	<u>$10,000</u>
Total debt payoff need (C):	*$305,000*

(D) Goals to be funded

College education for children:	$320,000
Contribution toward spouse's retirement need:	<u>$150,000</u>
Total funded goals need (D):	*$470,000*

Total life-insurance need (A + B + C + D): *<u>$1,290,120</u>*

[See Appendix 2 for a blank Life-Insurance Analysis Worksheet.]

The insurance need calculation can be useful in developing a general sense of the basic considerations for life insurance coverage requirements.

Although there are numerous types of life insurance products, life insurance can be classified under two basic categories: whole life and term life.

Whole Life Insurance

With whole life insurance, coverage is maintained for the "whole" life of the insured person. This type of insurance tends to be more costly because premium costs include the anticipated and eventual payment of a death benefit. This is true since the insured person is being insured for their "whole" life. There is a 100 percent certainty that death will occur and a payout will be required.

Term Life Insurance

With term life insurance, coverage is maintained on the life of the insured person for a certain period or term. This type of insurance tends to be less costly because a death-benefit payout is not certain. If death does not occur during the term of the insurance, the insurance company does not have to pay a death benefit and gets to keep the premiums received.

Generally, when a significant amount of life insurance is required, term life insurance is more affordable. For example, a young family with young children may need to insure the lives of the income earners for a period of twenty-one years, after which the children will have reached majority age. Significant amounts of coverage tend to be more cost prohibitive with whole life insurance.

Disability Insurance

The purpose of disability insurance is to protect against an interruption of income if a family member who helps support the family is injured and unable to work. If such an event occurs, disability insurance can replace up to 67 percent of income lost.

Obviously, the loss of a family member's income could harm the dependent family's financial situation. Failure to buy disability insurance could result in some of same severe economic hardships as would be present upon death. A few examples include:

➢ Family members can no longer afford to meet debt obligations, such as a mortgage payment and car payments.
➢ Family members can no longer afford normal living expenses.
➢ Family members can no longer pay for the children's education.

Two significant variables affect the cost of disability insurance premium cost: waiting period and benefit-coverage period.

Waiting period is the time between the disability event and the start of disability income payments. Waiting periods can be thirty days, sixty days, ninety days, and one and eighty days. Generally, the shorter the waiting period, the more expensive the insurance premium. The risk concern should focus on long-term disability lasting more than ninety days. It is long-term disability that would cause the greatest harm to financial wellness. In the short term, relying on emergency reserves would be best, thereby allowing for more affordable disability-insurance premium costs.

Benefit coverage period is the length of time disability benefits or income will be paid to the insured. These periods can range from thirty-six or sixty months to coverage for the lifespan of the insured. Generally, the longer the coverage period the higher premium. The risk concern should be to consider the time necessary for the family to adjust living expenses to a new norm and allow the insured to train for a new occupation if necessary.

Long Term Care Insurance

The purpose of long term care insurance is to protect against the risk of needing nursing-home care, home-health care, personal or adult day care as a senior.

For example, in recent U.S. News and World Report article, it was noted that an annual market survey performed by MetLife in 2010 revealed that the average monthly rate for assisted living communities was $3,293.

Needless to say the onslaught of such an expense could rapidly and completely deplete the financial and retirement assets that you worked so hard to accumulate over your working years. Failure to buy long term care insurance could result severe economic hardships. A few examples include:

➢ Family members may need to sell your home causing displacement
➢ Family members may have to consider a reverse mortgage thereby depleting equity in your home
➢ Family member may need to deplete your financial & retirement assets and perhaps their inheritance
➢ Family members may have to assist by providing financial support thereby affecting their personal financial situation

Securing long term care insurance would provide additional income should such care be required.

There four types of long term care costs: nursing home, assisted living communities, home-based care and adult day care services. Ensure that your policy provides coverage for each of the extended care cost needs.

Similar to disability insurance, premium will vary based on waiting periods and benefit coverage periods.

Although it may expensive to fully cover 100% of such cost, at least attempt to obtain a minimum amount of coverage to provide some financial assistance should extended care needs arise.

Conclusion

It is imperative to buy insurance to protect against death, and disability and long-term care risks. Failure to obtain insurance could result in negative financial consequences.

Action Steps to Improve Financial Wellness

1) Determine the amount of life insurance needed.

2) Take advantage of the maximum amount of life insurance available through your employer. Obtain additional private insurance if needed.

3) Determine the type of insurance best suited to meet your coverage needs and most affordable—for example, whole vs. term life insurance.

4) Take advantage of disability insurance available through your employer and or consider private disability insurance if necessary.

5) Consider the need for long term care insurance.

Simple Step #4: Work to Get Out of Debt

Much has been written and said about being in debt. It is certainly the most pervasive issue affecting our everyday lives. Managing debt is critical to overall financial wellness.

To manage debt, you must deal with both *debt coverage capacity* and *debt default risk*.

Debt Coverage Capacity

Managing debt coverage capacity involves making sure that income is sufficient to cover loan repayment requirements. Being overextended—not having sufficient income to meet debt payment obligations—would require you to divert money from other financial goals. Over a sustained period of time, inability to fund other initiatives could create long-term financial difficulty.

Debt Default Risk

Debt default risk is the probability of an event occurring that affects the borrower's ability to make required loan payments. In some instances, debt risk may have to be managed over a long period of time. For example, a conventional mortgage involves a repayment period of thirty years. Borrowers have to be concerned about the risk of default and must continually take steps—for thirty years—to protect themselves against such risks.

Debt risks are most acute when there is an interruption in the borrower's income stream. Below are some common events that interrupt income and potentially affect the borrower's ability to meet loan payment obligations:

➢ Job layoff or termination (involuntary and voluntary)
➢ Dependent spouse unable to return to work after children are born
➢ Starting a new business venture

Always Keep Working to Get Out of Debt

Think of debt as a temporary and short-term bridge to acquiring something. Debt can be used to get from the point of acquisition (Point A) to the point of full repayment (Point B). Move quickly between these two points by accelerating debt repayment. The longer it takes to get from Point A to Point B, the longer the exposure to debt risk.

Refuse to get over confident about your future earnings and ignore the risk of being in debt. Stay focused and vigilant on working to get out of debt.

In some instances debt can be used constructively when making significant purchases—such as a home or automobile—and paying for college. Appreciating some of the following concepts about debt can prove helpful in maintaining financial wellness.

High-Quality Debt

Debt used to acquire assets that have a future financial benefit fall under this category. The following items are examples of assets that have the potential for a future financial benefit:

- ➢ House
- ➢ College education
- ➢ Real-estate investments
- ➢ Business investments

Here are some examples of high-quality debt:

Type of Loan	_Reason Classified as High Quality_
Mortgage	Appreciating asset; interest tax-deductible
Student Loans	Income-producing (career earnings); interest tax-deductible
Business Loans	Income-producing; interest tax-deductible

Real-Estate Loans	Appreciating asset; income producing; interest tax-deductible

To summarize, these are the characteristics of high-quality debt:

- ➢ Related to appreciating assets
- ➢ Related to income-producing activities
- ➢ Interest tax-deductible
- ➢ Interest rates relatively lower than consumer debt rates

Low-Quality Debt

Debt used to acquire consumer goods that depreciate in value falls under this category. The following consumer goods depreciate in value:

- ➢ Automobiles
- ➢ Electronic goods
- ➢ Furniture
- ➢ Clothing

Here are some examples of low-quality debt:

Type of Loan	*Reason Classified as Low Quality*
Auto Loan	Depreciating asset; interest not tax-deductible
Store Accounts	Depreciating consumer assets; interest not tax-deductible
Credit-Card Debt	Depreciating assets; interest not tax-deductible

To summarize, these are the characteristics of low-quality debt:

> ➢ Related to depreciating consumer items
> ➢ Interest not tax-deductible
> ➢ Interest rates relatively higher

High-Quality Debt vs. Low-Quality Debt

Given the above characteristics of high-quality vs. low-quality debt, strive to minimize the use of low-quality financing. Excessive low-quality debt erodes financial net worth as you borrow at high interest rates to acquire consumer goods that depreciate in value.

Conversely, high-quality financing generally improves financial net worth by borrowing at lower interest rates to acquire assets that appreciate in value or assets that are income-producing. The return on investment in such assets tends to exceed the interest cost. The interest cost is further reduced on a net basis because interest is tax-deductible.

Getting Out of Debt

In order improve overall financial wellness you must make a sustained effort to manage and minimize financial exposure and the risks associated with debt. Over the long-term, there will be uncertainties and events that challenge financial stability and continued ability to meet loan payments. Develop a risk-adverse approach to debt and be aware that it is best to quickly move toward paying off debt and becoming free of debt. Getting out of debt will give you sufficient resources to meet other important financial goals.

Getting out of debt will take more time than it took to get in debt and will involve four key efforts:

1) Debt Assessment

For each debt owed, list:
➢ Creditor name
➢ Type of debt (credit card, auto loan, student loan, etc.)
➢ Minimum monthly payment requirements
➢ Amount owed to creditors
➢ Interest rate charged
➢ Current status (paid, past due, in collections)
➢ Obtain copy of your credit report to make sure the information it includes is the correct information for each debt.

[See Appendix 3 for Debt Analysis Worksheet]

2) Strategic Debt Repayment Plan

Determine your minimum debt-payment requirements and answer the following questions:
➢ Is your income sufficient to cover minimum debt payments?
  o If your income is not sufficient, what living expenses can be cut to balance the budget?
  o If your income is sufficient and a surplus exists, can the surplus be used to accelerate payoff of another debt?

[See Appendix 4 for Accelerated Debt-Repayment Strategy Worksheet.]

3) Change in Buying Behavior

Changing your buying behavior habits is paramount. Limit or discontinue the use of credit cards to make consumer purchases. Use cash instead. If sufficient cash is not available, delay the purchase until you have the money. Discontinuing the use of credit cards will help you to keep your debt levels from increasing and allow monthly payments to work toward reducing debts.

4) Sustained Focus and Commitment

Getting out of debt will take time. There is no instant solution. It requires sustained focus and commitment over a long period. Below is an approximation of the time it takes to pay off certain debts:

Credit cards and store charges	Three to five years
Auto loans	Four to five years
Student loans	Fifteen to twenty years
Mortgage loans	Twenty to thirty years

Action Steps to Improve Financial Wellness

1) Complete an accurate debt assessment

2) Develop a strategic debt-repayment plan

3) Change buying behavior

4) Sustain focus and commitment

5) Engage creditors and negotiate better terms.

Simple Step #5:
Live Within Your Means

To achieve Simple Steps #1 through #4, you will have to learn to budget. The goal of budgeting is partly to ensure monies are available to save for retirement, provide for emergencies, pay for insurance, and repay debt.

A budget is a strategic spending plan. In addition to achieving Simple Steps #1 through #4, a plan can also help keep spending within means (income limits).

Budgeting to Build Wealth

In a way, achieving Simple Steps #1 through #4 helped you to not only build wealth but protect it. However, if you don't keep to a budget, that building of wealth may not happen. Waiting until there is extra money left after paying bills won't work. Become unyielding about budgeting for wealth accumulation and savings. The budget line for wealth accumulation and savings is the most important item in the budget. Therefore, your strategic spending plan (budget) should start with setting aside money for wealth accumulation first.

Below are some of the basic vehicles that may be used for wealth accumulation:

➤ Automatic payroll deductions for deposit to an employee retirement account

➤ Systematic bank withdrawal for deposit to an IRA

➤ Systematic bank withdrawal for deposit to an investment account

➤ Systematic bank withdrawal for deposit to a savings account

➤ Systematic bank withdrawal for deposit to a FEMA (Family Emergency Management Account)

Balancing the Budget

After carving out a portion of the budget for resources earmarked to meet Simple Steps #1 through #4, the task is to balance the budget with the remaining resources.

First budget for *fixed* expense items and then separately for *discretionary* expense items. It is important to determine that there is sufficient income to cover fixed expenses. Subsequently, budget to afford discretionary expense items.

Fixed expense items in the budget include the following:

➤ Rent/mortgage payments
➤ Auto loan payments
➤ Auto insurance
➤ Credit-card payments
➤ Other loan payments
➤ Medical, life, and disability insurance
➤ Home utilities and maintenance

Discretionary expense items in the budget include the following:

- ➤ Auto repairs/gas
- ➤ Groceries
- ➤ Recreation
- ➤ Dry cleaning

[See Appendix 5 for a Budget Format Worksheet.]

Interpreting Budget Results

- ➤ If there is a surplus, consider using it to accelerate debt repayment.
- ➤ If there is a deficit, adjust discretionary expense items in sufficient amounts to at least break even.
- ➤ If a deficit still remains after adjusting discretionary expense items, investigate ways to restructure payment arrangements with fixed expense items.

Conclusion

Budgeting and the development of a strategic spending plan can help make sure expenses do not exceed income and have a negative effect on your ability to save for retirement, meet emergencies, and maintain important financial priorities. Without a strategic spending plan (budget), years of wealth and resources can easily pass through your hands into the treasuries of retailers, lenders, and the like. It is vitally important to manage resources in a manner that improves overall financial wellness.

Action Steps to Improve Financial Wellness

1) Use a budget format to evaluate your monthly income vs. expenses.

2) First, budget to contribute toward retirement, emergency savings, and risk protection (insurance).

3) Next, budget for fixed expense items.

4) Next, budget for discretionary expense items.

5) Determine appropriate action depending on whether there is a budget surplus or deficient.

Simple Step #6:
Plan for a Lasting Heritage

One of the most caring things you can do for your loved ones is to plan in advance to leave an orderly estate. We have all heard those dreaded words "They didn't have a will" and know the result can be chaos and more stress for grieving family members.

Estate planning is essentially advance planning of how assets are to be distributed upon death. A significant portion of assets can be distributed to heirs without the need to execute a will. This is because certain assets transfer upon death based on contractually designated beneficiaries. These beneficiary designations precede a will and dictate to whom assets are transferred upon death.

Below are some typical assets that transfer upon death to contractually designated beneficiaries and without the need for a will:

- ➢ Life-insurance proceeds
- ➢ Retirement assets
- ➢ Annuities assets

> ➢ Property owned as "joint tenants with rights of survivorship," which transfers to the surviving spouse-owner
> ➢ Bank accounts registered as "pay-on-death" accounts
> ➢ Investment accounts registered as "transfer-on-death" accounts

The above items sometimes constitute the majority of assets owned and transferred by most upon death. Therefore, estate planning can start immediately by reviewing beneficiary designation on the items listed above.

Below are some typical assets that would be benefit from executing a will to direct their transfer:

> ➢ Cash and savings accounts owned individually
> ➢ Investment accounts owned individually
> ➢ Personal property owned individually
> ➢ Real-estate assets owned individually
> ➢ Assets owned as a tenant in common

A Will

A will is the legal instrument made by an individual that directs how property is to be distributed upon death. The executor (personal representative) is the person named in the will to carry out the instructions of the will. If a person dies without a will, they have died "intestate." In such instances, the laws of the state the person resided in dictate how assets are to be distributed.

Some of the benefits of a will include:
- ➢ Person selects heirs rather than the state
- ➢ Person decides the executor of the estate
- ➢ Person selects guardian for young children

Conclusion

Thoughtful and careful consideration should be given to leaving orderly instructions to family members upon death. Such advance planning can help family members feel reassured and comforted in their loss.

Action Steps to Improve Financial Wellness

1) Review beneficiary designations on assets that can be distributed without a will.

2) Identify assets that need a will to be distributed.

3) Execute a will.

4) Identify the executor of your estate.

5) Store estate documents, life-insurance policies, and other important documents safely.

Simple Step #7:
File Income-Tax
Returns

The Internal Revenue Service (IRS) is a branch of the US Department of the Treasury. The IRS has some of the broadest sweeping powers and authority in the federal government. The IRS can seize property, garnish wages, file liens, and levy assets without court approval. The IRS's primary goal is to collect income taxes in order to provide the Treasury Department with the resources to finance the operations of the federal government. In fact, the IRS is likely to be the most significant federal authority many Americans will ever encounter. Given the IRS's mission and its sweeping power of authority, failure to comply with the filing requirements of the IRS can be extremely detrimental to overall financial wellness.

Some common penalties charged to taxpayers:

> *Failure/late-filing penalty* is 5 percent of the unpaid balance for each month or part of the month return is late, up to a maximum of 25 percent.

> ➤ *Failure/late-payment penalty* is .5 percent for each month or part of the month there is an unpaid balance, up to a maximum of 25 percent.
> ➤ *Interest on unpaid taxes* is the federal interest, which ranges from 6 to 7 percent annually.
> ➤ *Accuracy-related penalty* is 20 percent of under-payment attributable to negligence or disregard of tax rules and regulations.

File Tax Returns

Make a practice of filing timely income-tax returns. Mere filing of tax returns can help avoid the late/failure to file penalty, which could be as much as 25 percent of taxes owed. This type of penalty assessment is extremely harmful to overall financial wellness.

File Accurate Tax Returns

Tax laws are complex and ever-changing. It is important to prepare accurate tax returns, with correct application of tax laws. Returns filed based on faulty understanding and misapplication of the tax laws can result in an audit, changes to the return, and resultant penalties and interest. Negligence and disregard for tax rules can result in a penalty assessment of 25 percent.

File Returns Even If You Can't Pay

Even if there is a balance due, it is best to file the tax return. Just by filing, the taxpayer avoids the failure-to-file penalty, which can be as much as 25 percent of the balance owed. Furthermore, the taxpayer avoids the potential for a more severe charge by the IRS of income-tax evasion—failure to file a tax return. It is far better to file the return and work out a payment agreement.

Maintain Appropriate Support for Items Reported

The burden of proof is on the taxpayer. The IRS's position when examining a tax return is that it is the taxpayer's responsibility to substantiate or support all items reported on the tax return—not, as most people mistakenly believe, the IRS's responsibility to disprove them. It is important to maintain good records to support items reported on the tax return.

Conclusion

Filing timely and accurate tax returns will help maintain compliance with IRS regulations. Given the severity of enforcement actions available to IRS, full compliance will minimize any financial havoc that could be inflicted because of noncompliance.

Action Steps to Improve Financial Wellness

1) Routinely file income-tax returns.

2) File income-tax returns on time.

3) Appropriately apply tax laws in preparation of tax returns.

4) Maintain sufficient documents to support items on your tax return.

5) File returns even if you owe and can't pay.

Simple Step #8:
Know Your Investment
Risk

When investing in financial markets, the times are always turbulent because the markets can rise or fall suddenly and without warning.

Historically, there have been times when investment markets have experienced extreme volatility, causing some investors to experience substantial losses. Quite frankly, some investment assets may have to perform exceptionally well in the future just to recoup losses. When investing in the markets, maintain caution. It is critically important to know, understand, and manage investment risk.

Investment risk is defined as the chance that investment assets may decline in value. There is systematic investment risk and unsystematic investment risk.

Systematic Risk

This type of risk is caused by factors that affect the investment markets at large. Examples include changes in consumer prices and interest rates. Generally, changes in such factors affect most investments. It is not possible to eliminate systematic risk through diversification. These risks are also called *market risk or non-diversifiable risk*.

Unsystematic Risk

This type of risk is specific to an industry or firm. Examples of unsystematic risk include losses caused by changes in customer demand, new technologies, or labor problems. Assembling a diversified portfolio of investments can sometimes minimize unsystematic risk. A diversified portfolio would have multiple investments that react differently to the same set of economic circumstances. These risks are also called *diversifiable risk*.

Correlation of Investment Risks with Investments

To some degree, investment risk can also be correlated with the category of investment assets held. The three broad investment categories include:

- ➤ Stock investments (stock mutual funds, stocks)
- ➤ Bond investments (bond mutual funds, bonds)
- ➤ Cash investments (money-market funds, certificates of deposit)

Stock Investments

Stock investments consist of shares owned in a company and/or shares owned in a stock mutual fund.

Technically, owning stock means equity ownership in a company. Stock investments tend to fluctuate in relation to the state of the economy, the particular industry, and the specific company's performance. These factors are ever-changing, and so too are stock prices and stock investments. Stock investments are considered more risky because of the change factors and the potential for investment values to rise and fall rapidly. Stock investments may offer the potential for growth and higher rates of return than other investments.

Bond Investments

Bond investments consist of bonds owned directly or shares owned in a bond mutual fund. Bonds are debt instruments issued by a company or government agency that promises to pay a fixed rate of interest and return the investment at a stated maturity date. Bond investment values tend fluctuate inversely with fluctuations in interest rates. As interest rates rise, bond values decline. As interest rates decline, bond values increase. Although bond prices may fluctuate in value, the investment terms are fixed, and if the bonds are held to maturity, the full investment is returned. Additionally during the bond term the bondholder receives interest income payments. With bonds, there is also a default risk, which is the risk that the bond issuer will be unable to repay the investment. Bond investments tend to offer lower and steady rates of return on investments with less volatility in fluctuation of investment values than stocks.

Cash Investments

Cash investments include checking, savings, and money-market accounts as well as certificates of deposit. These investments are generally the most stable and have little to no fluctuations in values. They are have little to no investment risk. Interest earnings are stated and relatively low. Cash investments offer minimum rates slightly above the rate of inflation and stability of investment values.

Time Horizon

Understanding your time horizon is critical to managing investment risk. *Time horizon* refers to the time period between when the investing starts and when the investments are redeemed for use. The longer the time horizon (fifteen years or more), the more risk-tolerant an investor may be. The shorter the time horizon (five years or less), the less risk-tolerant.

A longer time horizon allows the investor to withstand short-term fluctuations, such as reductions in investment values, while pursuing a higher rate of return on investments in the future. Retirement investments generally fall into this category. Retirement may be fifteen or twenty years in the future, so fluctuations of investment values in the near-term are not as concerning. There is sufficient time to recover.

Stock investments may be suitable for investors with a longer time horizon. Although such investments tend to fluctuate in the short-term, they offer the potential for greater returns in the long-term.

When the time horizon is shorter, investments will need to be redeemed soon for use. More concern must be given to preserving the value of assets rather than return on investment. A shorter time horizon may not allow sufficient time to recover from a decline in investment values before there is a need to redeem investments. Persons nearing retirement tend to fall into this category. Retirement is near and reduction in investment values could have a dangerous effect on retirement plans.

Bond and cash investments may be suitable for investors with shorter time horizons. Although the return on investment tends to be less, these investments tend to be less volatile.

Investment Asset Mix Examples

Below are some ways to mix investments in consideration of particular time horizons.

Long time horizon—ten years or more (saving for retirement):

> ➢ Stock-oriented investments   75 percent
> ➢ Bond-oriented investments   25 percent
> ➢ Cash-oriented investments   0 percent

Medium time horizon—five to ten years (nearing retirement):
> ➢ Stock-oriented investments   10 percent
> ➢ Bond-oriented investments   75 percent
> ➢ Cash-oriented investments   15 percent

Short time horizon—less than five years (in retirement):

- ➤ Stock-oriented investments   10 percent
- ➤ Bond-oriented investments   65 percent
- ➤ Cash-oriented investments   25 percent

Conclusion

Investors should be aware of and understand the investment risks assumed in their portfolios. Consider the risk of loss in investment values—and how to mitigate it—when making investment decisions.

Action Steps to Improve Financial Wellness

1) Determine time horizon.

2) Classify investments under broad investment categories, such as stock, bond, or cash investments.

3) Determine the percentage weight of each investment category.

4) Review appropriateness of investment asset mix given time horizon.

5) Routinely reassess risks and appropriateness of investment mix.

Simple Step #9:
Invest in Education

Education is key to financial success. According to the US Department of Education, National Center for Education Statistics, in 2008 the median income earnings for young adults age twenty-five to thirty-five was as follows:

Young adults with master's degrees or higher	$55,000
Young adults with bachelor's degrees	$46,000
Young adults with associate's degrees	$36,000
Young adults with high-school diploma or equivalent	$30,000
Young adults without a high-school diploma or equivalent	$23,000

As these statistics show, in 2008, young adults who earned a bachelor's degree made twice as much as young adults who did not earn a high-school diploma, and those who went on for advanced degrees made even more. Evidence shows that investing in a college education may increase a child's future income potential. It is important to become well-educated in America; education has proven to be a key ingredient in financial success. Low-paying unskilled jobs tend to go to those who have invested least in education.

To help improve the financial future of their children, parents should invest their time, focus, and money in ensuring that their children are well-educated. Given the fast-paced, sophisticated, and technologically advanced society we function in today, striving to provide a college education for your children is the least you can do to establish their financial wellness.

Paying for College

It would be great if the goal of saving for college was easily realized. But having a pool of money set aside for college is tough given the day-to-day living expenses that most of us face. However, attempting to save something is better than nothing.

In addition to parents' out-of-pocket contributions, money for college tends comes from the following sources:

> ➤ Scholarships—awarded based on talent
> ➤ Federal grants (Pell grants)—awarded based on need
> ➤ Subsidized student loans—awarded based on need
> ➤ Unsubsidized student loans—awarded based on need
> ➤ Subsidized parent-student loans (Parent Plus Loans)—awarded based on need and credit
> ➤ Student loans provided by Sallie Mae—awarded based on credit worthiness

> ➤ Student loans provided by commercial lenders—awarded based on credit worthiness

Borrowing to Pay for College

There will be many loans that an individual will take out in his or her lifetime. There will be loans for the purchase of cars, clothes, electronic equipment, wedding rings, homes, and home improvements. Certainly, a loan to invest in a child's education and future earnings potential is one that should be considered prudent and feasible.

Below are the basic types of student loans offered and their loan terms.

Subsidized student loans. These loans are subsidized by the federal government and loan terms generally include the following:

> ➤ Interest rates are lower than unsubsidized loans.
> ➤ No interest accrues on the loan while the student is attending college full-time.
> ➤ No loan payments are required while the student is attending college full-time.
> ➤ Upon completion of school, if the student is unemployed or unable to start repaying loans, there are several deferment options.

Unsubsidized student loans. These loans are not subsidized by the federal government, and loan terms generally include the following:

> ➤ Interest rates are higher than subsidized loans.
> ➤ Interest accrues while the student is in school.

> ➤ No loan payments are required while the student is attending college full-time.
> ➤ Upon completion of school, if the student is unemployed or unable to make loan payments, there are limited deferment options.

Sallie Mae student loans. These loans are not subsidized by the federal government, and loan terms generally include the following:
> ➤ Interest rates are based on current bank prime rates.
> ➤ Interest accrues on the loan while the student is in school.
> ➤ No loan payments are required while the student is attending college full-time.
> ➤ Upon graduation, there are limited options for deferring loan payments.

Commercial bank loans. These loans are applied for and awarded based on the credit-worthiness of the borrower. The loan terms generally include the following:
> ➤ Interest rates are determined by the bank.
> ➤ Loan payments may commence immediately.
> ➤ Generally, no options for deferring loan payments.

If you'll need loans to pay for your child's college education, attempt to qualify for and maximize the use of subsidized student loans. If unsubsidized student loans are necessary, consider making at least the interest payment during the time the student is in school. If Sallie Mae loans are utilized, also consider making interest payments while the student is in school. Commercial bank loans should be the last source of financing.

Conclusion

Ben Franklin said, "Education pays the greatest dividends." He realized that the most important investment made is in one's education. With intellect and knowledge, an educated person can experience a return on investment in the form of higher earning potential for the future.

Action Steps to Improve Financial Wellness

1) Ensure children are well-educated for their future and consider a minimum of a college degree.

2) Begin to explore ways to reduce living expenses in order to meet out-of-pocket needs for paying for education. As the college years approach, consider deferring major purchases.

3) Reduce credit-card balances to lower monthly expenses and keep credit available if needed for education expenses.

4) Aggressively pursue scholarship opportunities. They are numerous.

5) Carefully consider lending sources for education.

Simple Step #10:
Avoid Ten Common
Financial Mishaps

Mishap is defined as an unfortunate accident. A synonym is *mischance*. Too often, people fall prey to mishaps in financial decisions that negatively affect their overall financial wellness. This chapter highlights ten common mishaps to avoid.

Early Distributions from Retirement Accounts

An early distribution occurs when money is withdrawn from a retirement account before the account holder reaches age 59½. Such distributions are assessed federal and state income taxes as well as a 10 percent early-withdrawal penalty. For example, assuming a federal tax rate of 20 percent, a state tax rate of 7 percent, and a penalty of 10 percent, the total tax and penalty assessment would be equal to 37 percent of the early distribution amount. Nearly 40 percent of the money withdrawn could be consumed by taxes and penalties.

Some distributions may be exempt from the 10 per-cent penalty:

➢ Distributions made because of total and permanent disability

➢ Distributions to meet qualified higher-education expenses

➢ Distributions for first-time homebuyers (no home ownership in prior two years)

Still, because of the hefty taxes, it's best to avoid early distributions except in extreme emergencies.

Failure to Make Payment Arrangements with IRS for Back Taxes Owed

The Internal Revenue Service (IRS) has powers of collection and enforcement that far exceed most creditors. The IRS can levy money in bank accounts, garnish wages, and file tax liens that damage credit ratings.

Often, a tax levy is the result of a taxpayer's failure to effectively manage and communicate with the IRS about delinquent taxes. A series of letters and even a certified letter will inform the taxpayer of a pending IRS enforcement action. Merely refusing to go to the post office to pick up the certified letter does not deter the IRS from progressing to more severe collection tactics.

It is vitally important to promptly respond to communications from the IRS and make acceptable payment arrangements. Qualified tax advisors may be helpful in negotiating payment arrangements.

Investing in Rental Property for
Tax Advantages

Investing in rental property should be based on economic factors, not tax savings opportunities. In fact, tax advantages from rental-property activity may be limited.

From a tax perspective if a taxpayer "actively participates" in rental activity, the taxpayer may qualify to deduct passive losses up to $25,000. However, this special loss allowance is reduced by 50 percent of the amount by which a taxpayer's modified adjusted gross income (AGI) exceeds $100,000. The allowance is reduced to zero when modified AGI reaches $150,000. Any unallowed losses are suspended until AGI is below the threshold or the property is disposed of.

Given that immediate tax benefits of owning rental property might be limited, primary consideration should be given to the economic merits of owning rental property. You should be able to answer yes to these questions:

➢ Is the property being purchased at a discount from the market value?

➢ Will the real-estate property appreciate in value? (Be realistic.)

➢ Will anticipated rental income be sufficient to cover the mortgage and property expenses?

➢ Is there expertise available to manage, maintain, and repair the property?

➢ Are there adequate financial reserves to meet any unexpected property issues?

Don't believe the press that rental property is a good tax-savings strategy. Invest in real estate based on economic factors.

Transferring Title to Assets
Before Inherited

One of the most ill-advised tactics is to transfer the title of property to a future beneficiary prior to the death of the donor. Doing so can have very negative tax consequences.

When a beneficiary inherits a property pursuant to death, the beneficiary receives a stepped-up tax basis in the asset inherited. That means the beneficiary gets to establish a new tax basis in the asset inherited equal to the fair-market value as of the date of death. If a property is transferred prior to death, the beneficiary receives the donor's basis in asset inherited.

Below are examples of the difference in tax treatment.

Assumptions
Owner's basis is a stock portfolio: $10,000
Owner's value of stock portfolio at death of death: $100,000
Beneficiary's proceeds upon sale of inherited stock portfolio: $105,000

Stepped-up tax basis to the beneficiary

Proceeds from sale of inherited stock portfolio	$105,000
Beneficiary's stepped-up basis in stock portfolio	$100,000
Taxable gain	*$5,000*

No stepped-up tax basis to the beneficiary
Proceeds from sale of inherited
   stock portfolio $105,000
Beneficiary's basis in stock portfolio   <u>$10,000</u>
    Taxable gain   *$95,000*

Under the "stepped-up tax basis" treatment the taxable gain would be $5,000. Without "stepped-up" tax basis, the gain would be $95,000. The benefit of a "stepped-up" tax basis is significant. Be patient and wait to inherit assets and benefit from stepped-up basis.

Purchasing Annuities near Retirement

When purchasing annuities, concern should be given to liquidity given age of the purchaser. Annuities have restrictions on withdrawals and surrender fees may be charged if withdrawals exceed annual limits. Persons nearing or in retirement have a greater probability of making withdrawals to meet retirement needs and could potentially incur surrender charges.

For example, assume an annuity product has an annual withdrawal limit of 10 percent for the next ten years, and the principal investment was $100,000. The purchaser of the annuity would be limited to withdrawing $10,000 annually. Withdrawals in excess of $10,000 would be subject to surrender charges. In the first year of an annuity product, surrender charges could be as much as 7 percent.

Very careful consideration should be given to the suitability of annuities, given their withdrawal limitations.

Buying vs. Repairing a Car

Too often, when repairs start mounting on an old car, the most convenient alternative is to buy a new car to replace it. When a major repair is required, do the math before running out and buying a new car. Compare the cost of the repair to the annual cost of twelve monthly car-note payments. If the cost of the repair is less than the annual cost of twelve monthly car payments, it may be more economical to repair the car. Too often, the thinking is to get rid of the car before it has little to no value. Here again, though, compare the cost of twelve car-note payments to what might be lost in trade-in value. If the cost of annual car-note payments exceeds the loss in trade-in value, it may be more economical to keep the car. The dealer will always be willing to give you something for your trade-in. Additionally, having a period of time when you are relieved of a monthly car payment will allow monies to be used to meet other financial goals.

Cosigning a Loan

In essence, the lender has determined the risk of default for the borrower is so significant that an additional, more credit-worthy person must be secured as a backup. That additional security is a cosigner. The cosigner is providing insurance against default for free and upon default becomes just as liable as the original borrower.

In the event that the borrower fails to pay, the lender can actively pursue the cosigner as if he or she were the original borrower. Additionally, failure of the cosigner to pay will have a negative effect on the cosigner's credit rating.

The best-case scenario is to avoid cosigning. If cosigning is necessary, make sure there is financial capacity to assume the liability in case of default by the original borrower. Unexpectedly becoming liable for someone else's debts can be very damaging financially.

Filing Bankruptcy to Seek Creditor Relief

Bankruptcy can be a very effective tool under certain circumstances, such as protection against lawsuits, seizure of assets, and foreclosure. However, too often bankruptcy filings are used merely to stop creditors from calling and hassling for collections.

Bankruptcy will have a negative affect on your credit for many years. For example, a Chapter 7 bankruptcy can remain on your credit report for up to ten years. Bankruptcy may make it extremely difficult to get a mortgage if you don't already have one.

Before filing for bankruptcy, first determine which creditors are secured and which are unsecured. If the major concern is secured creditors, consider trying to negotiate satisfactory payment arrangements. With respect to unsecured creditors, seek the assistance of nonprofit credit-counseling organizations. These organizations can be strong advocates for working out payment arrangements with various unsecured creditors. If lawsuits arise, consider contacting the attorney and negotiating payment arrangements. However, in order to effectively negotiate payment arrangements, you must have a budget. Creditors tend to respect an arrangement that is supported by budget figures.

Finally, bad credit is still better than having a bankruptcy filing listed on your creditor report. Given the severe consequences of filing bankruptcy, it should be used in only the most severe cases.

Divorce Litigation

Too often, parties with modest resources fail to resolve divorce conflicts amicably. As a result, the parties incur significant economic loss due to exorbitant legal fees and inequitable settlement arrangements, not to mention the emotional cost.

As the parties continue to argue and mistrust each other, legal fees extract and drain what modest economic resources the parties had. At the end of the litigation process, a judge, who least knows both parties, decides their fate. The judge splits the assets, divides up the family in ways perhaps neither party imagined, and goes home at the end of day to his or her family and says, "Honey, what a day I had in court." The lawyers are fairly compensated for their work, and the divorcing parties are left financially and emotionally bankrupt.

Resolving financial issues equitably can lead to a peaceful resolution of the other matters in a divorce. Mediation sessions with qualified advisors can help the parties to gradually come to the middle and negotiate difficult matters.

"Get Rich Quick" Schemes

If it sounds too good to be true, it probably is. Such schemes tend to play on Americans' hopes of becoming a millionaire. They offer great promises of wealth that appear to defy other limitations experienced in everyday life. As stated in the introduction, most Americans will never become millionaires. However, it is possible to enjoy a wealthy and healthy financial lifestyle. Money is truly made the old-fashioned way: you earn it. Avoid falling prey to such schemes, which may fraudulently take your limited hard-earned resources accumulated over years.

Consult with trusted advisors and friends who can offer an objective and grounded perspective on questionable endeavors.

Conclusion

Nonroutine financial matters require greater research and careful consideration. Be sure to make well-informed decisions. Often, good planning is simply making the best choice given adequate information. This chapter attempts to highlight some of the more common planning issues that need additional thought to avoid common mishaps.

Conclusion

There is an old proverb that states, "the conclusion of a matter is better than the beginning of the matter." I trust that after reading this book, you feel better about your financial future than your past. I hope that you believe in your ability to take simple yet significant steps to improve your financial wellness.

Futhermore, I trust that you have concluded the following:

> ➤ While being a millionaire may be a lofty goal, the goal of improving your overall financial wellness is very attainable.
>
> ➤ The steps presented to improve overall financial wellness are rather simple and not extremely sophisticated.
>
> ➤ Some steps you can start immediately.
>
> ➤ Being more aware of common financial pitfalls will help protect you against making bad financial decisions that affect your overall financial wellness.

I believe that we are all entitled to a measure of financial prosperity. With each level of financial wealth comes challenges, from the least to the greatest. The difference is successful execution of basic fundamentals. If the simple steps highlighted in this book are performed most excellently you will experience an improvement in the overall financial wellness.

Thanks for reading this book. It is truly an honor to know that my ideas may help readers improve their overall financial wellness.

As you implement some of these simple steps, I would love to hear from you and chronicle your results. Please feel free to email me at info@kevinhutt.com or visit my website at www.kevinhutt.com.

Remember, begin today!

I sincerely wish you all the best,

K. Thomas Hutt, CFP®, CPA, MBA

Appendix

Appendix 1:
Retirement Analysis Worksheet

(A) Retirement assets needed

Annual gross wages:	$_____
Less federal tax withholding @ ___%:	($_____)
Less state tax withholding @___%:	($_____)
Less social security tax withholding @___%:	($_____)
Less medicare tax withholding @___%:	($_____)
Annual after-tax income:	$_____
Estimated percentage needed in retirement*:	x_____%
Annual retirement-income need:	$_____
Multiplied by number of years in retirement:	x_____
Total retirement assets needed (A):	$_____

(B) Amount expected from Social Security

Estimated annual Social Security:	$_____
Multiplied by number of years expected to receive benefits:	x_____
Total assets from Social Security (B):	$_____

(C) Additional retirement assets needed (A-B): $_____

*Generally, 75 percent of after-tax income is estimated to be needed in retirement.

Determining the amount of monthly savings required to meet additional retirement assets needed: Below is a simple approach to estimating the monthly savings amount required to meet additional retirement assets needed:

(C) Additional retirement assets needed (A–B):	$_____
Number of years remaining before retirement:	/_____years
Annual savings need:	$_____
	/_____months
Monthly savings need:	$_____

Appendix 2:
Life-Insurance Analysis Worksheet

(A) Income-replacement need

Annual gross wages:	$_____
Less federal tax withholding @ ___%:	($_____)
Less state tax withholding @___%:	($_____)
Less Social Security tax withholding @___%:	($_____)
Less Medicare tax withholding @___%:	($_____)
Annual after-tax income:	$_____
Estimated percentage needed by family members:	x_____%
Annual income needed	$_____
Multiplied by number of years until	
youngest child is 21:	_____
Total income-replacement needed (A):	$_____

(B) Funeral and estate-administration need

Funeral expense:	$_____
Estate administration:	$_____
Total funeral/estate-administration need (B):	$_____

(C) Debt-payoff need

Mortgage balance:	$_____
Credit-card balances:	$_____
Auto-loan balances:	$_____
Other debts:	
Total debt-payoff need (C):	$_____

(D) Goals to be funded

College-education cost for children:	$_____
Contribution to retirement needs:	$_____
Total goals-funded need (D):	$_____

Total life-insurance need (A + B + C + D):	$_____

Appendix 3:
Debt Analysis Worksheet

Home Mortgages			
Creditor Name	Monthly Payment	Balance Owed	Interest Rate
Total home mortgages:			

Credit Cards			
Creditor Name	Monthly Payment	Balance Owed	Interest Rate
Total credit-card debt:			

Auto Loans			
Creditor Name	Monthly Payment	Balance Owed	Interest Rate
Total auto loans:			

Investment Loans			
Creditor Name	Monthly Payment	Balance Owed	Interest Rate
Total Investment loans:			

Student Loans			
Creditor Name	Monthly Payment	Balance Owed	Interest Rate
Total Student loans:			

Home Mortgages *(continued)*

Pay-Off Date	Account Number	Contact Information

Credit Cards *(continued)*

Pay-Off Date	Account Number	Contact Information

Auto Loans *(continued)*

Pay-Off Date	Account Number	Contact Information

Investment Loans *(continued)*

Pay-Off Date	Account Number	Contact Information

Student Loans *(continued)*

Pay-Off Date	Account Number	Contact Information

Appendix 4:
Accelerated Debt-Repayment Plan

Step 1: Discontinue use of credit cards, except in emergencies.

Stop using credit cards immediately. This step ensures that debts are no longer increasing and that making regular payments will start to reduce debt levels. There is no need to necessarily close the accounts because they may be needed in case of an emergency.

Step 2: Prepare a monthly budget to generate surplus.

A monthly budget will help you determine the amount of monthly surplus or deficit. If there is a deficit, first work to get to a break-even point where expenses equal income. Determine what expenses need to be reduced. After budget improvements result in a surplus, determine the extra amount available to accelerate paying off of debts.

Step 3: Pay off credit cards and store accounts.

The first point of attack is to pay off low-quality debt obligations. These debts include credit cards and store accounts. Use the extra amount available and focus on paying off the account with the lowest balance. Selecting the account with the lowest balance will result in a quicker payoff and a sense of accomplishment. Once the account with the lowest balance has been paid off, use the standard payment plus the extra amount that was being added and apply it toward the account with the next lowest balance. Continue this strategy until all credit cards and store accounts have been paid off.

Step 4: Pay off auto loans.

Use the total amount now available from paying off credit and store accounts to accelerate payoff of auto loans. After the auto loans have been paid off, set aside a portion of the savings for future repair or replacement needs.

Step 5: Pay off student loans.

Use the total amount now available after paying off credit-card accounts and auto loans to apply toward student loans. Here is where the children can help out. If the college-educated child is gainfully employed, consider requesting his or her assistance in accelerating payoff of student loans. By accelerating payoff, financial resources can now be used by the parents to accelerate paying off the mortgage.

Step 6: Pay off the mortgage.

After paying off other debts, use the total amount now available to apply toward paying off the mortgage.

Appendix 5:
Budget Format Worksheet

Net take-home income (after taxes)

Income source 1:_____ $_____

Income source 2:_____ $_____

Income source 3:_____ $_____

Income source 4:_____ $_____

                        Total income: *$*_____

Major Expenses

Rent/mortgage: $_____

Auto loan payments: $_____

Auto insurance: $_____

Credit-card payments: $_____

Other loan payments: $_____

Home utilities: $_____

Medical/life/disability insurance:

                    Total fixed expense: *$*_____

Discretionary expense

Auto repairs/maintenance: $_____

Auto gas: $_____

Groceries: $_____

Recreation: $_____

Dry cleaning: $_____

Clothing: $_____

Grooming: $_____

Vacationing: $_____

Other: _____ $_____

Other: _____ $_____

Other: _____ $_____

Other: _____ $_____

            Total discretionary expense: *$*_____

                    Net surplus (deficit): *$*_____

www.ingramcontent.com/pod-product-compliance
Lightning Source LLC
Chambersburg PA
CBHW031325290526
45784CB00014B/2135